Tommys Girl

Stories of the High Country...

Stories of my Life...

**A book of poetry by
Lee Taylor-Friend**

Published by High Country Press
P.O. Box 946
JINDABYNE NSW 2627
Ph: (0408)166-200
www.leetaylorfriend.com

For permission to reproduce, store, transmit or perform any part
of this book, please e-mail: leetaylorfriend@hotmail.com

PHOTOCOPYING

Please keep in mind that photocopying threatens the viability of
future re-prints. Please help our small press by recommending this
book to family and friends and sharing the inspirational stories of
the 'High Country' people of the Snowy Mountains, Australia.

National Library of Australia Cataloguing-in-Publication Data:
Creator: Taylor-Friend, Lee., 1968- author.
Tommys Girl : Stories of the High Country...Stories of my Life...
ISBN: 9780646478425 (Paperback)
ISBN: 9780994429032 (Print On Demand – CreateSpace)
Subjects: 1. Taylor-Friend, Lee., 1968- - Poetry.
2. Snowy Mountains (N.S.W.) - Social life and customs - Poetry.
Dewey Number: A821.4

Cover photography by John Taylor
Cover Design by Kerry Beer Photography and High Country Press
Proof read by Marie McGrath and Jean Gamon
Text typesetting/design/formatting: Patricia Adams and HCP
3rd edition printed by Blizzard Publishing, Jindabyne, Australia.

Disclaimer
All care has been taken in the preparation of the poetry herein, but
no responsibility can be accepted by the publisher or author for any
damages resulting from the misinterpretation of this work.

About the Author

Lee Taylor-Friend is a Mother, poet, writer, support worker, remedial massage therapist and presenter of 'writing as therapy workshops' living in the picturesque Snowy Mountains Region of Australia with her Husband, two sons and a menagerie of animals on a small property just outside Jindabyne.

Lee is well known in her local community and volunteers her time for a variety of community events, local committees and causes.

Lee wrote her first poem in 2004. She became mesmerized by the tales of the local Snowy Mountains men and women and was inspired to tell their stories through 'Bush' or 'Rhyming Poetry' - a great Australian tradition.

This has led to wonderful connections and great friendships with many of the people she has written about.

Lee, 'The Poet from Snowy River', has been widely published and won many awards.

'Tommys Girl', Lee's much anticipated first book of poetry, was originally released as a paperback book in 2007 with two successful print runs selling out.

This is the third edition. Enjoy!!

Acknowledgements

I would like to thank the following people for their encouragement, support and inspiration.

Firstly, the wonderful men and women who have shared their stories and memories with me. You are acknowledged by name throughout this book.

Those who encouraged me to publish my book 'Tommys Girl' back in 2007 including Shaaron Ellis, Stumpy Pendergast, Robert and Carole Thomas.

My Friends and Family who encourage and support me.

I would like to thank my wonderful Husband and our boys Ben and Jake for their understanding, support of my literary endeavours and unconditional love.

Last but not least I give unending thanks and praise to my friend and mentor 'Jinda Jean Gamon'. If not for your constant encouragement and enthusiasm for my work I suspect I would have given up writing long ago…

Lee T.F.

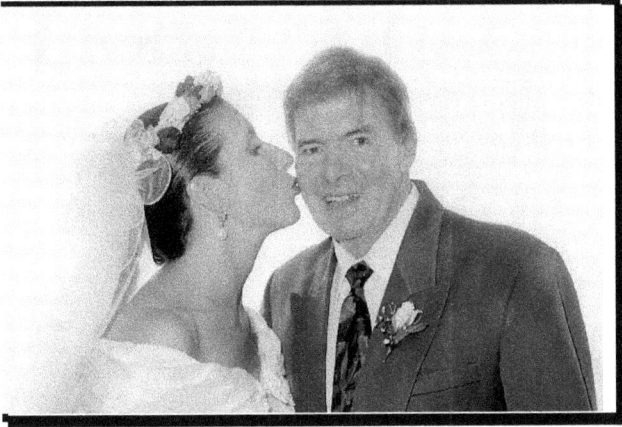

Dedication

I dedicate this book to my late Father

Thomas 'Tommy' Friend.

(b. 8.8.33 - d. 23.12.96)

Thank you for passing on 'a love of the verse'

for being such a good Father and a great mate.

Forever in my heart...

Contents

Tommys Girl

I remember just like it was yesterday.
The laughter, the fun times we had.
We'd jump on the old Sydney ferry.
Two girls and Tommy, their Dad.

On a Sunday we'd all go down fishing.
Ride the ferry from Circular Quay.
We'd mostly go over to Old Cremorne Point.
We'd catch bream and leathers for tea.

In those days life was pretty simple.
Old handlines and schoolies for bait.
We'd bus it or walk back to Redfern.
We mostly got home pretty late.

Back then Sydney wasn't a city so much,
It was more like a 'country town' then.
You knew all your neighbours, looked out for each other,
You knew who was foe, who was friend.

Well, I know that it wasn't that easy,
To raise two young girls on his own.
Mum was real crook in the hospital.
It was rare she was ever at home.

I didn't learn knitting or sewing,
Or other more 'womanly' skills.
But what my dear Father did teach me,
My head and my heart it still fills.

He taught me to always be honest.
Best policy bar none he'd say.
To be kind, strong and true, and listen more too,
And don't suffer fools on the way.

He taught me to hammer a nail.
He passed on a love of the verse.
The gift of the gab, well that came from Dad,
But probably that one's a curse!

There are so many things that he taught me,
He sure was a true rarity.
But the love and compassion he showed one and all,
That's what I hope sticks with me…

He raised and he guided throughout teenage years,
No doubt, quite a challenge at times.
Allowed me to make some mistakes of my own,
To ponder life's reasons and rhymes.

He was there as I journeyed to young adulthood,
Finding my way in the world.
Searching for all of life's meanings.
Changing to woman from girl.

I now think of those days so fondly.
My Father, my mate and my friend.
I learnt so much, we laughed, we cried,
But I guess all good things have to end…

I fear that you left this world early,
You'd only just turned sixty-three.
But you know that you could have been nine score and ten!
It would have been too soon for me.

I fancy you're up at the 'Pearly-Gates Inn',
That heavenly tavern on high.
Having a beer and a laugh with your mates,
Family and friends by your side.

Standing with arms about Mother.
Singing an Ol' Blue Eyes song.
I'm glad that you both are together again,
I know that it's where you belong…

But no matter where my life may lead me,
In this fickle and funny old world.
The roads that I'll travel, still yet to unravel,
I'll always just be 'Tommys Girl'.

Ode to Good Neighbours

It was back there in 2000 that we moved to Jindabyne,
We thought we'd have a 'sea change' but, well, of the mountain kind.

We packed up our belongings, left behind the city strife,
And travelled to the country, just a Husband and his Wife.

We've had some grand adventures, made great mates along the way,
It's two of these 'real special' friends I'll talk about today.

Well Bill and Elle were neighbours on the property next door,
But then as time went passing they became a whole lot more.

Elle became my friend and mother all rolled into one,
A confidant, a great support when I had my first born son.

Her warmth, her joy, her happiness, that true serenity,
She taught me how to oil paint, brought out the best in me.

Bill, well he's a top bloke, a trouper through and through,
Found a brown snake in the chook house, well what was I to do?

He said 'Got a long-necked shovel?' in his West Virginian drawl,
'I'll knock the damn thing on the head, no problem at all!'

Years go by and times they change and people must move too,
They've gone up North 'semi-retired', to start their life anew.

So thank you for your friendship, Bill and Elle Burnett,
We'll have a beer, say 'cheers!' to you, I'm mighty glad we met!

Before I go, an anecdote, just one thing more to say,
We've taught young Ben if he sees a snake just run, run, run away!

But sometimes he says with a questioning look and alas to my dismay,
'If I see a snake I'll run, run, run, but Mummy Bill can stay!'

The Ballad of Tin Mine Falls

Story telling is an integral part of the 'Aussie' character. The incomparable Banjo Paterson poem 'The Man from Snowy River' ignites a passion in many a heart and identifies us as a nation both here and abroad. I was lucky enough to spend time with some of our true 'Men from Snowy River' and 'local legends' - Ossie Wellsmore who made it to the ripe old age of 100 years! And brothers Jack and Mick Pendergast – all of whom have sadly since passed on. They shared many of their fabulous yarns and stories with me.

Many of the stories they did share were in turn told to them by older stockmen when they were young men! Their capacity for detail and marvellous memories never ceased to amaze me. The following poem is based on the recollections of Jack Pendergast, as told to him by the late Jack Freebody. It is set in the late 1920's and is a tale of true courage, selflessness and determination to save the life of a stranger…

In high country remote where the eucalypt soar,
Where the sun barely touches the steep forest floor,
Is a place so majestic, that wilderness bore,
That place is called Tin Mine Falls.

To harness such beauty, a rare thing to do,
A prize to be captured, yet done by so few,
Two men came from Melbourne, their challenges grew,
To photograph Tin Mine Falls.

Their guides led them in on a trusty bush horse,
Through bushland so rugged, a treacherous course,
Edging closer they heard her sheer power and force,
The magnificent Tin Mine Falls.

Her beauty revealed, quite a sight to behold,
Over four hundred feet to the bottom I'm told,
No one could foresee dramas yet to unfold,
Mesmerised by the Tin Mine Falls.

Ever closer he edged, perfect photo to take,
Engrossed by their splendour, that was his mistake,
On the dirt, lost his footing, his life now at stake,
He fell over the Tin Mine Falls.

Big Jack Pendergast rode through the dead of the night,
To put out the call of a man and his plight,
So far to Benambra by pale moonlight,
To warn them of Tin Mine Falls.

He finally made it, sweat dripped from his brow,
He put out the call for the police to come now!
He had to get back, keep an unspoken vow,
To save him from Tin Mine Falls.

Also to Jindabyne, word had got through,
Of a man who had fallen, a rescue to do,
The sergeant of police and Jim Woodhouse went too,
They rode out for the Tin Mine Falls.

Coming in were Dave Spencer and Jack with their cattle,
They knew Jack should go; it would be quite a battle,
By the Pinch and the Jacobs, he turned in his saddle,
So well he knew Tin Mine Falls.

Jack Freebody answered and heeded the call,
Rode bushland so rugged, sure death if you fall,
Many miles to go, there was no time to stall,
Must get back to Tin Mine Falls.

Determined, they rode at one hell of a rate,
Raced like men possessed, hoping they weren't too late,
No way to predict or determine his fate,
They made it to Tin Mine Falls!

On a ledge with a wattle tree, nowhere to go,
His features pale ghostly, the light fading low,
Grabbed the ropes, rug and halter, must bring him up slow,
To the top of the Tin Mine Falls.

They looked over the falls, what a treacherous course!
Police unsure what to do; they looked on with remorse,
Jack thought to himself, 'they ain't fit for the force',
He went over the Tin Mine Falls.

He secured him well with the halter and rope,
They brought him up slowly; they prayed he could cope,
With Jack Pender at top, there was plenty of hope,
They got him up Tin Mine Falls.

Quite fiercely, the wind then blew in from the west,
Must get him some shelter, some tucker and rest,
Make sure that his wounds were all cleaned, set and dressed,
A night camped at Tin Mine Falls.

His leg and his jaw had been broken quite bad,
Fixed with green bark and horsehair, whatever Jack had,
The bush his dispensary since a young lad,
Bush doctor at Tin Mine Falls.

What could save this young man, it was well understood,
Was to drink all the milk and the Bovril he could,
Fed through rolled up green bark, his jaw broke mighty good,
His life saved at Tin Mine Falls.

They took him out slow on Jacks' trusty pack horse,
Bags of tussock tied on her to cushion the force,
That sturdy old steed took a sure footed course,
Rode away from the Tin Mine Falls.

At the Limestone Creek waited an old wagonette,
Must get him to town and a hospital yet,
The journey near finished, their challenges met,
Back safely from Tin Mine Falls.

They got him to Melbourne, somehow he'd survived,
Those magnificent Bushmen, they'd struggled and strived,
They'd risked their own necks just to keep him alive,
Those heroes of Tin Mine Falls.

Then many years later, a message came through,
From a doctor in Melbourne, who'd treated him too,
'What a mighty good job that fine bushman did do!
All those years back at Tin Mine Falls.'

So this is a tale, though true it sounds tall,
Of remarkable Bushmen who heeded the call,
Though these legends have passed, it's their deeds I recall,
In the ballad of Tin Mine Falls…

To Feel the Pinch

This was my first serious attempt at writing poetry. On entering my first competition, I was thrilled to win 2nd place at the 2004 Snowy River Festival. The closure of vast tracts of National Park has had a huge impact on horse riders. Thankfully, the Pinch River riding area was saved. Many others were not…

Down in the Lower Snowy, where the gum trees soar and sway,
Is the great south boarder of the park they want to take away.
The silence can be deafening, the serenity surreal,
Down by the old Pinch River, well, it has a special feel.

They rode for generations, through this wild and untamed land,
Their Fathers, Sisters, Brothers, with a trusty steed at hand.
The heritage, the history, well that will never change,
For nothing is more natural than riding on the range.

Plan of Management (POM) you say the impacts too adverse,
But all the tourists in four wheel drives; you tell me which is worse?
Then there's the feral animals, a problem through and through,
They're mostly found on four legs, but sometimes on just the two!

When a search and rescue can't be done by 4WD or chopper,
They'll ride on in and save the day when KNP come a cropper.
It's hard to have it both ways, but when called they'll come along.
For no true Aussie worth their salt can stand a whinging POM.

The more you close, the less to ride, the problem can you see?
To back them in a corner, will 'impact adversely'!
We all must work together, a solution must be found,
You can't just lock the public out and call it hallowed ground.

This vast and priceless beauty should be all of ours to share,
For future generations to enjoy without a care.
But those who ride and know her you bet they won't budge an inch!
For to ride her is to love her and to really 'Feel the Pinch'.

17 Horses & 17 Men

From The Recollections of Ossie Wellsmore

17 horses for 17 men
Went riding out that day.
17 horses for 17 men
A river to survey.

A feat of engineering.
But a price we'd have to pay.
To quench the thirst of many.
The Snowy lost her way…

They first rode by 1919
Past Paupong school that day.
Just a boy I watched them.
Down Snowy River way.

Returning 1938
Grand planning to portray.
They stayed for good this time.
A permanent foray…

I was the one that led them out
But I was led astray.
17 horses for 17 men
The river was taken away…

A feat of engineering.
But a price we'd have to pay.
To quench the thirst of many.
The Snowy lost her way…

If only I'd have known
The price we'd have to pay
I'd have taken the buggers out
And let the horses stray…

History & Heritage
Legacy & Legend

I wrote this poem after a great weekend at the 2005 Snowy River Festival, Dalgety, NSW.

Men and women, living legends, in these mountains and beyond,
Many of you are among us here today.
Your trials and tribulations, your stories told with pride,
Ever etched into our hearts and minds they stay...

For this place becomes a part of you, its branded on your soul,
With every ridge and gully that you ride.
As you recall deeds and heroics, such awe inspiring feats,
When you rode so boldly on the great divide.

This legacy and legend that our forbearers created,
Are the ones we try to keep alive today.
The stories, yarns, bush poetry, skilled riding, stockman's challenge,
Whip crack, dog jump, bullocks in the dray.

I've heard it said our heritage is fading with the years,
And it's true all things in life evolve and change.
But I saw first-hand the passion and the heritage still thriving,
With the young and old arriving,
At the Snowy River Festival that fine November day...

I watched you led by kin so proud; as you'd navigate the gathering crowd,
In chairs with wheels and spokes of gleaming steel.
I saw people stop to shake your hand, for you are legends of this land,
To celebrate your heritage, how proud it made me feel...

And I thank you for the stories and the yarns you've shared so freely,
With this girl who hailed from down Sydney way.
I've a passion for this land in which my Grandfather was born,
It's the place I now belong and where I know I'll always stay.

We will gather once again this year to celebrate our culture dear,
I'll watch your smiles, your laughter and your sighs,
And though much in life will come and go
and change with passing years I know,
I'll always see those memories reflected in your eyes...

The Day the Fires Came...1939

While many people are familiar with the 2003 fires, the great fires of 1939 had an enormous impact on communities that was felt for many years afterwards.

This remarkable tale of survival against the odds is written through the eyes of Don who was a child of just four years old. This poem won first place at the 2005 Snowy River Festival.

FROM THE RECOLLECTIONS OF OSSIE & DON WELLSMORE

A blistering, scorching day, we were caught up in the fray,
In the way of an unstoppable great fire,
Taking all within its path, waiting for the aftermath,
Fear and loathing now of natures wrath, the flames were soaring higher…

Two days and nights we battled, on foot and in the saddle,
Just chaff bags soaked in water trying to keep the blaze at bay.
No choppers then or planes, no fire trucks, no rain,
No rest, no sleep, no time to stop, we fought her night and day.

The scorching wind, terrific, consequently, quite horrific,
Our home for generations now, these mountains that we love.
Hills and valleys, open plains, Snowy River, raw terrain,
Unforgiving, unforgettable, we prayed to God above…

The heat was so intense, livestock perished by the fence,
The enormous strain of fire and heat, it left its deadly brand.
The pressure was so great; man or beast would not escape,
Fighting on defiantly, we had to make a stand…

It was in mid-afternoon, with intensity and gloom,
The fire was right upon us now, she held us in her grip.
There was nowhere left to shelter from the searing heat and swelter,
We would have to take our chances and take cover in the dip.

For those who do not know, it is where the sheep must go,
To rid them of the maggots, that infest the wool and skin.
Pure arsenic mixed with water, felt like lambs into the slaughter,
Our only hope of shelter, or the fire would surely win.

We were over by the gate, then with a twist of fate,
The fire appeared from nowhere and came roaring up the road.
We surely did take fright; Dad came running into sight,
He grabbed us, one under each arm, toward the dip he strode.

There were ten or twelve inside, in that arsenic water tide,
The men still on the outside, pouring water overhead.
For the fiery wind so hot, it would take the flaming lot.
If we didn't keep the water up we'd surely burn instead.

A kangaroo dog, he jumped in, to save his scalding skin,
A hunting dog, quite greyhound like, and almost whippet thin.
We filled up every space; fear possessed our hearts, our face.
Women, children, baby boy, neighbours, friends and kin.

Then the baby caught alight, what a bleak god awful sight!
No time to think or hesitate must act and act damn quick.
Dad grabbed the nearest pail, doused the babes flames without fail,
But within the pail not water, but pure foul arsenic...

That baby turned bright yellow, in the stinking sheep dip shallows,
The flames were out! The baby boy, his life was surely saved!
His mother washed him off in the arsenic water trough,
No time for self-admonishment we had to all be brave.

Uncle Chris dropped to his knees, praying for a last reprieve,
Down below the house, the fire came and burnt him off the post.
'Well bugger ya' he said, 'I'm not planning to be dead',
He ran back to the stables then to let the horses go.

I was on Grandmother's knee, embers flying so fiercely,
They would fall and burn her arms that held me safe within the dip.
She would grimace with the pain, in the scorching ember rain,
But not once did she dare loosen her protective vice-like grip.

In the confusion smoke and heat, came the words hard to repeat,
'Is my house gone?' Grandma asked, and simply 'yes', came her reply.
Her head dropped in defeat, teardrops glistened on her cheek,
It's the only day I ever, ever saw my Grandma cry...

The fire passed overhead, thought that we were surely dead,
Like a freight train it went roaring with such power heat and force.
Then everything went still, body tingled, spine it chilled,
The fire had passed us over; we'd survived its deadly course.

When we slowly did emerge, from the arsenic water scourge,
Surreal, such desolation, we'd escaped a fiery hell.
A stranger then appeared, from the paddock, singed and seared,
He made it to the water tank and then collapsed and fell.

Grandpa fought a gallant fight, for two full days and nights,
Side by side with all the men, he took the hits and dives.
But a mighty price he paid, had a heart attack that day,
Fading in and out of consciousness, he'd surely saved our lives.

Other men dropped where they stood, they had done the best they could,
Had they just collapsed exhausted? Firestruck? We did not know.
We poured water overhead, prayed to God that they weren't dead,
We hoped we could retrieve our car then into town we'd go.

Some luck had come our way; our car was saved that day,
Our Dodge was in a dried out dam and somehow it was spared.
We all climbed or clambered in, arsenic burning on our skin,
A dishevelled, beat-up, barefoot lot, but no one really cared.

We headed then for town; no one moved or made a sound,
The searing heat and savagery, it took enormous toll,
The cattle and the sheep, hooves were dropping from their feet,
No land untouched, all obsolete, our livelihood it stole…

Buckley's Crossing now not far, in the safety of our car,
We drove to meet the others who survived that fateful day.
We arrived at the hotel, quite a sight and quite a smell,
The veranda full of country folk who'd all escaped the fray.

Some eyes squinting, some grew wide, no hiding their surprise,
No way to get a message through, so onto town we'd pressed.
Some were neighbours, some were friends, doing double take again,
They could not recognize us we were such an awful mess!

They kindly took us in, truly treated us like kin,
They fed and clothed and washed us and the bush nurse, she came too.
Eyes were bathed, our wounds were dressed, we all needed sleep and rest
The nurse took care of Grandpa, did the best that she could do…

When we ventured home again, our lives forever changed,
The loss was so enormous, we would rebuild with regret,
To survive through such a fire, natures giant funeral pyre,
It is something neither man nor beast could ever soon forget…

Our small home had not burnt down, but when we had a look around,
A hole in our veranda burnt, a dinner plate in size!
But it didn't catch alight, quite amazing in hindsight,
So we all moved in together, to the task ahead we'd rise.

So many stock had perished, blackened earth, the land we cherished,
The fences, livestock, homestead gone, now years of work ahead.
We battled on determined, to defeat that fiery vermin,
We rose up from the ashes to rebuild our lives instead.

The thing I most remember, from the day of falling ember,
Were the piles of white bleached bones, where livestock perished by the
fence. They remained that way for years, through the blood and sweat
and tears, Stark reminders of that fateful day, the memories intense.

Unforgettable for me, 'twas my birthday too you see,
Mother made a special birthday cake, left cooling on the tray.
But while they checked our houses fate, the men ate half my cake!
Well, I guess no one was game to light a candle on that day…

Some my memories, some were told, from a bygone day of old,
Our lives were changed forever by that January day…
Grandma's house gone, Babe in flames, Grandpa never quite the same.
But, you know that Babes an old man now, and still alive today!

Many years have come and gone, still our legacy lives on,
Seven generations now, our passion, time can't quell.
Then January zero-three, fire struck again you see,
And my son now has a fire story of his own to tell…

It's a hard life on the land, and we all must lend a hand,
Through fire, feast or famine, your resolve must never wane,
Still the images can haunt me; they can paralyse and taunt me,
Etched in my memory still remains the day the fires came…

The day the fires came…

The day the fires came…

The Day the Fires Came...2003

This poem is based on the story of Kerry Wellsmore (son of Don), and his brother-in-law Mark Troha. Similarities to the 1939 experience some sixty-four years earlier were astounding, if not a little eerie...

No breath of wind had touched the hills for many days before,
The land stood shrouded, thick with smoke and haze.
We knew that rain would save us and we hoped against all hope,
But the smoke and ash persisted now for days...

We rode out to survey, put in fire breaks that day,
We guided in the dozers, hoped our efforts weren't in vain.
Hills and valleys, open plains, Snowy River, raw terrain
Our home for generations, our resolve could never wane.

The wind picked up a little, as we shifted in our saddle,
A nor-wester now, no life within her fiery, burning gape.
For as fast as man may travel, over fallen logs and gravel,
On horseback one would surely not outrun her or escape...

Then the wind it turned quite fiercely, circumspect, the heat was piercing.
We pulled left on our bridle, turned their heads, for home we stole.
But the fire she followed racing, there was surely no out-pacing,
We would have to take our chances, head toward the waterhole.

We were riding for our life, through the searing heat and strife,
It was surely right upon us and we rode like men possessed.
Over mountain rough terrain, 'till we found our feet again,
Edging closer to that waterhole, hearts thumping in our chest.

As I glanced over my shoulder, old fates hand could not be colder,
A wall of flames was soaring, ghost-like licking at my heels.
Falling ash felt like a sickle, thinking life can be so fickle,
Hurdling burning brush and embers, maybe this is how hell feels...

We were racing nip and tuck, both beseeching lady luck,
Flames were gaining on the uphills, horse and rider on decent.
We were racing now to shelter from the searing heat and swelter,
The waterhole not far now, it was surely heaven sent.

We dismounted and took cover, as we prayed for one another,
Our trusty steeds would have to run to save their mountain hides.
Such horses prized immensely, as I thought and wished intensely,
Though the horse took me to water, how I hope that he survives.

Like a mirage, we waded in, water lapping at our chin,
Then the fire, like a freight-train, it went roaring overhead,
The power, heat and strain, our bodies gripped with pain,
The inferno, right upon us, thought that we were surely dead...

In the silent passing wane, we had found our life again,
From the bitter burning ashes, we emerged from our cocoon.
To survive through such a fire, natures giant funeral pyre,
It is something neither man nor beast could ever forget soon...

Now sometimes I stare and listen, as the snowflakes fall and glisten,
And my baby boys and wife lay gently sleeping in their beds,
I can see the smoke and flame, and I'm taken there again,
Back to a place, that no-man's land, still living in my head.

It's a hard life on the land, and we all must lend a hand,
Through fire, feast or famine you'll stay loyal all the same,
Still the images can haunt me; they can paralyse and taunt me,
Etched in my memory still remains, the day the fires came...

The day the fires came...

The day the fires came...

Autumn Leaves

The autumn leaves are falling,
Gently floating to the ground,
Evoking strong, sweet memories,
Of sight, and smell, and sound.

A menagerie of colour, light,
And energy on high,
I watch them dancing on the breeze,
So joyously they fly…

Such rich and vibrant imagery,
Against azure skies,
Orange, red and aubergine,
They capture heart and eye.

A glistening graceful canopy,
Of amber, yellow, gold,
So many autumns come and gone,
Such stories to be told…

A time now for reflection,
Strength and beauty's all I see,
As winter snow approaches,
And the autumn slowly leaves…

Tommys Girl

The Stockwhip on the Wall

The following poem is the first I ever wrote about 'My Mate Jack'. On our numerous trips to the Snowy Mountains over the years, my husband and I would often stop off at the Bredbo Pub for a beer and a bite to eat.

Among the many iconic items of yesteryear hanging on the wall of the pub was a stockwhip. Apparently the very one I wrote about in this poem! Thus, I finished the poem and called it "The Stockwhip on the Wall".

A few years back all items were removed from the walls of the pub for painting and put in storage. It was assumed the whip was amongst them but after much searching, the stockwhip was never found…True to the history of this whip it has gone 'walkabout' yet again but if anyone can confirm its whereabouts, please, give me a call…

It is a very special whip, I'll tell you about today,
It's had a chequered, coloured past, or nine lives some might say,
It travelled over mountain tops, wherever Jack would roam,
It seems to me this whip took on a life all of its own!

A stockwhips a possession prized, as any stockman knows,
It speaks a special language; your bond to whip it grows.
A good old four strand greenhide can't beat a whip like that!
When you get her going there's a fearsome mighty crack!!!

I want to tell a story of a whip of some repute,
A corker of a tale that I'm sure none will refute.
It was told to me by 'Jack', who's quite a legend in his time,
He told me in his own words, now I pray that he likes mine…

'Twas the first whip that he made when he came back from the war,
No doubt it was a blessing to be back on our fine shore…
He'd been up 'round the Currango with a wiry mob of sheep,
But he had to go to Sydney town, a repat check to keep.

While he was up Sydney way this story did unfold,
Enough to make a mans' blood boil and turn his heart real cold.
Three blokes from up the big smoke came; well, one was quite the joker,
Two were called 'solicitors' and one a 'hotel broker'!!

The broker went into the stable and grabbed Jacks' whip and saddle,
But luck old Tom Taylor came before he could skedaddle.
The broker said 'I'll pinch Jack's whip', and cracked it like a lout.
'I'll hang it on the hotel wall for all to talk about!!!'

Well you see, Tom Taylor heard this and he said what came to mind,
'That whip belongs to my mate Jack; you'll do nothing of the bloody kind!
Put it back there where you found it, you should not have it out'.
I'd say that broker bloke was blessed he didn't cop a clout!

'If you ask Jack, real nice I add, he might just make you one,
But don't let him know what you did today, or he might just shoot you son!'
Jack made the whip as promised and it went down Bredbo way,
To hang on the wall, a prize possessed, its legend grew each day.

Many years later Jack's brother Dave, went droving down that way,
His mates took him into the Bredbo Pub, a little visit they did pay,
'Where'd you get that stockwhip from', said Dave with a glint in his eye,
'A bloody old fella up the mountains made it', came the manager's reply!

Well some are now in Canada, some in the USA.
The Aussie stockman's hall of fame has one or two they say.
The one the broker nearly flogged, well that's in Melbourne now.
Jack's stockwhips live Australia wide, their craftsmanship renown.

I went to Bredbo recently, sat down, I had a beer,
I glanced around and there it was! I grinned from ear to ear…
It hangs up there with pride of place, as seasons rise and fall,
Made by one Jack Pendergast, the stockwhip on the wall.

My Mate Jack

...an ode to Jack Pendergast

Life often leads on journeys
Down an unexpected track.
You think your 'sailing' one way
When you take a different tack.

Fate led me to a meeting
On that special April day.
It turned my life 'full-circle'
In a funny kind of way...

It's many years since we first met,
Though I felt we'd met before.
Friendships that span the 'bridge of age'
Enlighten so much more...

We've shared some very special times.
Much humour, the odd tear.
And on our trip to Oldfield's Hut
We even shared a beer...

You've told me stories of a past
That few will ever see.
Fine anecdotes that touch the heart.
Thank God that laughter's free...

Well truth's stranger than fiction
You've proven that to me.
Your yarns and precious memories
Have become 'sheer poetry'...

You've had your final muster now,
But still I think of you.
Reflecting on amazing times
And hardships that you knew...

A larrikin whose smiles and laughter
Always brought me back.
My life's been enriched enormously
Because of 'MY MATE JACK'...

Through Her Eyes

...an ode to Hoppy Webb

A woman, slight of stature, yet strong and mountain bred.

Infectious smile, laconic laugh, proud carriage of her head.

She stopped and had a yarn a while and kindly offered tea.

We reminisced of days gone by when life was hard, but free...

With one eye always on the mob, she swung upon her horse,

And boldly rode the open plain through tussock grass and gorse.

She wheeled her beast 'round to the left and safely bought him back.

Amongst his mob 500 strong who roamed this stock route track.

From 'Califat', the family home in Adelong they came,

Droving cattle down to 'Yaouk' for the summer feed and rain.

This track her mother travelled, and her mother before her,

Bush country filled with memories that uplift, haunt and stir...

On the Tumut-Yaouk stock route many travelled to and fro,

Now they'll close this page of history because 'parks' say 'time to go'.

To some perhaps, its names on maps, a stock route they despise.

But how I wish for just one day they'd see it through her eyes...

Across the Tumut River, Argalong and Roast Beef Creek,

Past Emu Flat to Sassafras, such beauty here to seek...

The history at Broken Cart where miners panned for gold,

The rattling chains of spirits past can still be heard I'm told...

A creek named Never-Never and past Tin Pot Flat too,

Then on to Big Mount Peppercorn, an awe-inspiring view.

Nearbys', the Murrumbidgee running out of Fiery Range,

But first you'll travel by Long Plain with history sad and strange...

You'll see a solemn grave site where Frances Dunn is lain,

Her parents, too, passed droving but their memories remain...

A place to stop and say a prayer, reflecting on the past,

How can you tell a daughter, that this trip may be her last?

There are huts and creeks and gullies, a rivers' lazy bend.

A thousand different stories as they've roamed from end to end.

A path much travelled, much revered, still, some don't understand,

Hearts stay entwined forever with this sacred, rugged land...

Now as I watch her riding through this land she loves once more,

I fear this time could be her last, for who knows what's in store?

But before 'parks' make decisions that are binding and must stand,

Please, reflect upon this story, for her life has been this land...

Breaking of the Drought?

The drought is still having such a huge impact on rural communities, particularly with rising rates of depression and suicide...
This poem was written after a good drop of rain and reflects the stoic resilience of those on the land whom I admire greatly.

Wild, torrential rains are falling
From a sodden misty sky.
Swallowed greedily and guzzled
By the parched earth where she lie.

For the rain so seldom cometh
And we all began to doubt
That we'd ever see the breaking
Of this God-forsaken drought.

Tarnished land is looking greener
As the paddocks come to life
To sustain the farmer's weaner
And to halt impending strife.

If the manna come from heaven
In the manner that we pray
Then the sky will show some mercy
And deliver every day!

See, the farmers' life's a hard one,
At the peril of the sky.
Gale force winds, and heat then blizzard
Many ask the question 'Why?'

But the farmer simply answers:
'Mate, we'll see the hard times out
For it has to come eventually...'
'The breaking of the drought'.

Bush Country Bush Country…

Bush country, bush country,
You capture the dawn.
Transparently floating
Through mist covered morn.

Entranced by your beauty,
Enshrined in your fold.
Bush country, bush country,
My spirit you hold…

Bush country, bush country,
You call me at night.
Your whisperings echo 'cross
Pale moonlight.

Alive in the darkness,
Such mysteries to seek.
Bush country, bush country,
What wisdoms you speak…

Bush country, bush country,
Look kindly on me.
Instil your fine virtue
Of humility.

Enlighten and guide me,
Your ways I behold.
Bush country, bush country,
Your lessons unfold…

Bush country, bush country,
My love and my life.
You've given such solace
Through turmoil and strife.

You silently counsel,
My true voice I share.
Bush country, bush country,
My heart I lay bare…

Bush country, bush country,
You talk to my soul.
Your intimate calling,
My ultimate goal.

To be in your presence,
To whisper to thee.
Bush country, bush country,
My spirits set free…

An Angel Amongst Angels

...an ode to Mick Pendergast

The three brothers mentioned in this poem are the late Mick, Jack and Dave Pendergast. I was fortunate to share many a yarn and conversation with Mick and Jack. This particular story really touched my heart. Mick was a man of few words yet the ones he did speak were powerful and poignant. At the end of WW2 food was scarce. Mick told me they were under instructions not to feed the locals – the 'Fuzzy-Wuzzies' or as they were fondly known 'The Fuzzy-Wuzzy Angels' for their many heroic deeds helping soldiers in Papua New Guinea during WW2. Mick secretly supplied food to the local people in need and no doubt saved many lives himself – that's why I called this poem 'An angel amongst angels...'

Mick passed away 16th March, 2007, aged 93 years.

I felt compelled to write this poem not only as a tribute to Mick, Jack and Dave, but to all who have fought in, lived through or experienced war. This and every ANZAC Day 'We Will Remember Them'.

From Australia's Snowy Mountains, back in 1942,
Three brothers left to go and fight a war.
They were sent up to New Guinea where their challenges then grew,
To fight a foe upon a strange new shore.

They marched a trail formidable; they called 'Kokoda Track',
They saw their share of hardships 'long the way.
But then as fate would have it half way up, they turned them back,
Thank God, 'twas not their destiny to stay.

They marched back down the way they came, three days or so it took,
Passing those who'd fared much worse, with every stride.
They were posted to Port Moresby then where Mick was made the cook,
Often sleeping, working, eating side-by-side.

There are many things these brothers felt, experienced and saw,
Snipers bullets, sinking boats and wounded crew.
And it's often hard to talk about the things you've seen in war,
But you'll 'soldier on' and 'do what you must do'…

But Mick, he went beyond this, with the kindness that was shown
To the locals, without food at the wars end.
They would crouch behind the steel mesh, amongst them it was
Known that this cook was now a saviour and a friend…

The compound was surrounded by a fence with razor wire,
And the 'Fuzzy-Wuzzys' gathered there at night.
He would hand food out to one and all, of this he'd never tire,
And they'd savour any tucker with delight!

It was only scraps and leftovers, whatever he could find,
He'd add vitamins and then he'd water down.
It wasn't flash or fussy, but their bellies were all lined,
And he'd try to make enough to go around.

After eating this for two weeks, he could see them coming good,
They regained the strength and sparkle in their eyes.
And he was content in knowing he had done all that he could,
Still, he found it mighty hard to say 'goodbyes'…

From adversity came kindness, such selflessness from strife,
From this humble mountain man of words so few.
What he gave the 'Fuzzy-Wuzzys' was the greatest gift - their life
And they surely found an angel, Mick, in you…

Snowdrifts of Time...

Based on the story of Mrs Tommy Thompson who went missing in the great snowfall of 1949. As told by Jack Pendergast.

The snow continued falling in a constant wall of white,
It had done so now for many, many days.
With the pantry all but empty, no blizzards end in sight,
And the fire just a soft, slow burning haze…

The bitter winds were blowing through the crevices and cracks.
The children huddled trying to keep warm.
Their bellies in a hungry knot, the winds chill on their backs,
As they waited to see out this endless storm.

Father looked forlorn at Mother, she would have to ride,
They knew that the horse could not take Father's extra weight.
Their trusty steed was old and poor her riding days now few,
Still, he felt it should be him, at any rate.

She'd ride some miles from West Lynne Road to Grosses Plain to call
And return with what provisions she could find.
Mrs Thompson, small of stature, but with courage she stood tall,
As she rode on with a singleness of mind…

The wild storm was raging; the conditions mighty grim.
It was hard to see your hand before your face.
But the horse led on so boldly, while risking life and limb,
For she sensed her way, so well she knew this place.

But when many hours passed and Mother had not made it back,
Her Husband had to make that dreaded call.
To report a wife feared missing made his heart and mind turn black.
Too much to bear, to lose, no time to stall.

A message came for Jack to go and see if he could find this
Woman that her family held so dear.
He'd been moving stock since sun up but he didn't at all mind,
For you'll fight to save a friend and show no fear.

'Twas hard to tell in dark of night, with tracks now worn so deep,
If she'd come this way, or if she'd made it back.
So he rode on out to find her, a solemn vow to keep,
As he headed down a cold and stormy track.

He rode a mile toward the creek he knew that she must cross,
Convinced that she would travel but one way.
'Tween the safety of the culvert and the fence she'd pass across,
And from this path he was sure she'd never stray.

The wild wind was howling as the dark of night set in.
The snow and sago whipped and burnt his face.
The matches struck were useless, so he knew he must begin
To dismount and feel for tracks he hoped in place.

And then perchance he found them! His hand carefully read the snow.
Jack could feel the horses hoof prints pointing down.
She'd travelled home; he knew this by the imprint of the toe,
His job was done; he mounted and turned 'round.

So this family was spared the grief of losing one they love.
A Husband held and thanked God for his Wife.
Children hugged and kissed a Mother, a true gift from up from above.
And a Mother simply gave thanks for her life...

And the man who rode to save her on that cold and bitter night,
Sat to have a nip of rum and bowl of stew.
He was just content in knowing that she'd made it home alright,
For it could have been much worse, he surely knew...

Such men and women now epitomise the character of those,
Who have made these mountains what they are today.
For without that kind of 'mateship' we'd be nowhere I suppose...
Through 'snowdrifts of time' this testament will stay.

A Trip To Remember…

Oldfields Hut, 21 November 2005

Each year our council organise a fabulous four wheel drive trip for 'The Boys from Snowy River'. Luckily, I have got to tag along and was inspired to write the following two poems to remember our journeys…

We rounded up at Berridale that fine November day,
The sun shone mighty brightly as we headed on our way.
With 43 fine mountain men and volunteers 14,
We headed for a special place that I had never seen…

The cavalcade impressive! There were four wheel drives galore,
The posse slowly headed out, well what a day in store!
Through Middlingbank we travelled, past Adaminaby,
A right turn then to Yaouk past the glistening 'Murrumbidgee'.

We stopped for 'morning tea' and Everett Oldfield met us there,
His home, his hospitality, so kindly he did share.
The countryside just magic! So green and lush and fair,
The yarns and laughs flowed freely; we didn't have a care…

Then back on board our 'horse with wheels' and up the track we went.
A fire trail through rough terrain, a hair-raising ascent!
Through hills and streams and valleys, this well-worn road was cut,
But finally, we made it to the famous 'Oldfields Hut'…

An open plain enveloped us, she held us in her fold,
Hills and mountains rose above us in this land so strong and bold.
'Oldfields Hut' the crowning glory, timbers rising up to heaven
So masterfully created back in 1927…

A splendid time was had by all, with talks and poetry,
Mr Oldfield shared his knowledge of such rich and fine history.
The view was just magnificent, the hut a sight to see,
Great food, great yarns, great company, nowhere I'd rather be…

Stories flowed, and memories shared, no doubt some memories made,
But finally we had to go, a fond farewell we bade…
Then heading home we stopped off at a very special place,
To see 'Currango Homestead' put a smile on every face…

We travelled by Tantangara Dam, to Adaminaby,
Farewelled some very special mates then 'homeward bound,' you see,
A marvellous day was had by all, a 'perfect' trip I'd say,
And I hope I'll be invited to your next 'Big Men's Trip' Day!!!

We're Going to the Snowy…

Men's 4WD Trip, 2 November 2006

We're going to the 'Snowy', we're heading out today,

We're going to the 'Snowy', we're packed, we're on our way!

A sturdy stream of four wheel drives are headed down the road,

Packed to the brim with 'Mountain Men' all in 'adventure mode'.

We passed across Dalgety Bridge, we all are 'Paupong Bound',

Such sweeping, graceful landscape, yet parched and thirsty ground.

The grey clouds gathered overhead, oh how we prayed for rain,

But not until we'd had our trip and made it home again!!!

The first steep trail we travelled in a single ordered file

But when we made it to the top we had to stop a while…

Such snow-capped splendour on the range, far as the eye could see,

All sculptured by 'the hands of time', ours for posterity.

We ventured next to Rugman's Hut, we stopped off and explored,

This little 'piece of heaven' that they've re-built and restored.

With rough sawn timber memories of times and travels past,

Reflecting on the 'droving days' through bushland wild and vast.

Now back on board our 'horse-with-wheels' we made our way on down,

To the sacred 'Snowy River', a jewel in this precious lands crown.

We admired her breathtaking beauty, remembered her powerful past.

We reflected on poor Charlie Rugman, his '43 crossing his last…

We walked 'long the banks of the river, meandered through soft river sand,

Some talking and some just reflecting, remembering life on the land.

We ate and we drank, we were merry to sit and reflect with a mate,

Tales of river in flood and of droving when the Snowy was mighty and great.

But alas, we could not stay forever for the weather looked ominous and grey.

So we packed up our camp and our cargo and we headed on our 'merry way'.

Up and down over hills over mountains, ups and downs like the journey of life,

In the safe hands of Mr Vaughn Pender, I was sure that he'd keep us from strife!!!

'Many thanks', once again, for the invite to a wonderful annual event,

I've experienced part of our history, great yarns and such special times spent.

'Homeward bound' and we travelled a trail that was rough as a blokes

three day growth.

If you asked "Would you travel this path once again?" I'd just answer "Well yeah",

"BLOODY OATH!"

The Simple Life

I stare out at the scribbly gum,
The chooks, the vegie patch.
There's nowhere that I'd rather be,
Nowhere could ever match...

You can take your great big mansions.
Your castles in the sky.
Designer clothes and flashy cars,
They all go by the by.

Material possessions.
Accumulated wealth.
Do they truly make you happy
Or just compromise your health?

The more some get, the more they want,
Or that's the way it seems.
To keep up with the 'Joneses',
It's a life filled with pipe dreams...

Contentment seems so elusive.
True happiness so hard to find.
But booze, drugs or pills won't cure your ills,
And they sure won't heal your mind.

We must get our priorities sorted.

Back to basics and work it from there.

Most lives have got too complicated.

Need to look deep within if you dare…

But perhaps I should not be judgemental.

We all have our own way, our own path.

It just seems my keen observation,

Most could cut all their stresses in half!

I guess it's just what we get used to.

Some really do enjoy the stress.

The trappings that wealth and success bring,

For some they do really impress.

I am sure that my life in the country,

would seem quite horrific to some!

Fencing and weeding, cleaning chook poo and breeding,

Enjoying just being a Mum…

So I guess we will just have to differ,

I'll take my life simple and free.

And you will take yours, with eloquent pause,

All I'll say's "Thank god it's not me!"

The Blessing

I stare out at the scribbly gums,
Listen to cicadas songs,
The bore brings water slowly,
And the birds they chime along.

The creaking and the groaning,
As the sunlight bakes the shed.
The vegie patch it glistens,
The smell of baking bread.

My baby boys lay sleeping,
Softly breathing, warmly dressed,
This is my reality,
For which I'm truly blessed.

As gently he awakens,
I hold baby to my breast,
A life so dear and precious,
I hold baby to my breast...

The Brave Old Warrior

I was riding up to 'Kosi' on a friends old mountain bike,

But half way I got tired, it was really quite a hike!!!

I stopped, sat and admired the majestic mountain view.

A time for quiet reflection, such a peaceful moment too...

A stranger then came walking by, we stopped and talked awhile,

He shared knowledge, laughs and stories and he'd walked many a mile,

Through this wondrous, rugged landscape as he'd done for many years,

A lone and brave old warrior with little time for fears...

From Sydney to the mountains he'd come time and time again,

To walk up to Mount Townsend through such stark and wild terrain,

Past hut and hills and valleys ever onwards he would roam,

It seemed to me that in his heart this truly was his home...

He taught me things about this place that I had never known

And though we finally parted ways, a part of me had grown...

But his final words were priceless, inspirational I'd say,

"I've come here for my birthday, see, I'm seventy today!!!"

How Great Thine Art

...an ode to Alan Grosvenor

I was asked to write the following poem by Noeline, the artists' wife, as a tribute and to celebrate her husband's 81st birthday. She told me about their life together and her heartfelt desire for Alan to be recognised for the amazing contribution he has made not only to the Snowy Mountains, but the art world at large.

There was much laughter and a few tears that day and I thank Noeline for asking me to write this poem. I sincerely hope it goes a small way towards paying Alan Grosvenor the thanks and respect he deserves.

Alan painted close to 6,000 pieces of art during a career spanning over 60 years with 42 of those years spent here in the Snowy Mountains. Alan generously donated many of his works to charity to raise funds for a variety of worthy causes. Alan passed away in 2012 at the age of 86.

Six thousand visions of beauty.

Six thousand pieces of gold.

Six thousand lives changed forever.

Six thousand stories are told...

Such glorious imagery hanging

In gilded halls here and worldwide.

Portraying our 'High Country' splendid.

Exuding such beauty and pride...

A life filled with colour resplendent.

In mist tones of every fine hue.

A lifetime of love and devotion.

Strength and passion in all that you do...

The bold, fluid movement of horses,

Embraced by the falling of snow.

The mystical magic of sunset.

A fiery night sky all aglow…

Brush strokes from the hand of a lover

And a country's true beauty unfurled.

These visions and moods of the mountains

So endearingly shared with the world…

By a man who has travelled nigh six thousand paths,

Lived with challenges, triumph and change.

A man who has given so much of himself,

Who has captured the heart of 'The Range'…

Six thousand visions of beauty.

Six thousand pieces of gold.

Six thousand lives changed forever.

Still, many more to be told…

Tommys Girl

History Repeats...

Whilst this poem is not written about any one person, there is a common thread that runs through the vein of this story. When I ask many of the older men I speak with 'What was your Father like?' the answer is often 'He was a hard man' or occasionally 'He was a hard old bastard'...
This poem is a reflection of those sentiments...

My dad was a tough and sombre man,
As hard as this rugged land.
From the earliest time I remember,
'Twas my duty to lend a hand...

From sun-up until sundown
I worked hard as any man could.
Determined to make my old Father proud.
Young hands calloused with wire and wood...

There was no need for formal schooling
From the time that I turned thirteen.
'Twas the harsh school of life I attended
And through drought years, such hardship I've seen...

My Mother raised twelve able children,
In a cottage just three rooms of stone.
Father mostly was working or drinking.
It was often she raised us alone...

As the eldest it became my duty
To make sure that the farm was still run.
Father's tongue lashings became more frequent
As did beatings because of the rum...

Father died and the children all grew up.
Mostly married and went their own way.
The farm was my life and my duty.
Mother's too, so with me she would stay.

The years passed and I married my sweetheart.
Dear Jeannie, the love of my life.
She bore me three sons and five daughters.
A hardworking, honest, good wife.

But such praises, I found hard to tell her.
Instead my tongue lashed like nine whips.
Filled with anger and words unbecoming
Grog fuelled fury would pour from my lips.

Work and drinking were blurred and life busy.
My sons toiled as their Father had done.
From the age of thirteen they would work
Just like men from the dawn till the setting of sun.

Then the boys went to war for their country.
The girls married and they moved away.
Too much for one old man to farm on his own.
Too much for wife Jeannie to stay...

My dear Jeannie has left me for heaven.
My eight children have now become six.
Three boys went to war, only one returned home.
Such a loss even time cannot fix...

As I sit and reflect on my memories,
Just A few shared and many untold...
The enemy 'time' will be coming
And my unearthly fate will unfold...

I declare if I had my time over
I would change my harsh manners and ways.
I would tell my dear wife that I love her.
Praise my children the rest of my days...

I see clearly from time spent reflecting,
We should learn from mistakes of our past.
Who knows when words spoken to others
May be words that just might be our last...

But my wrongs they will never be righted.
Years of harshness cannot be undone.
My biggest regret, unbeknownst to me,
My own Father is who I'd become...

See, our family and loved ones are precious
And time, in an instant she fleets.
We must heal to avoid the mistakes of the past
for the sayings true... 'HISTORY REPEATS'...

Don't Sell Our Snowy Hydro!

The following two poems are a bit like 'Bookends' to me. This poem started my involvement in the fight to stop the sale of Snowy Hydro whilst 'Never give up' was written on the day the sale was stopped, and what a fight it was! I likened our home to being like a bunker, on the go 24/7 running a full-blown media campaign and organizing protest rallies from our living rooms! It was a truly remarkable experience and a great reminder that by coming together for a common cause, for the greater good, we, the people can achieve great things.

They came from countries far and wide

To build the Snowy Scheme.

They left behind the 'scars of war'

To build Australia's dream…

A 'melting pot' of cultures

All working side by side.

They toiled through conditions harsh,

They did it all with pride…

Whole towns were moved to 'higher ground',

Farms buried 'neath the lake.

The 'Mighty Snowy' lost her flow

And many a heart did break…

A 'feat of engineering',

The 'dream to end all dreams'.

But now it seems its being sold,

Yet no-one heeds the screams…

How can politicians promise?

That 'all will be O.K.'

For 'assurances' get broken

And the people always pay…

Water is a precious resource,

And one that we must keep,

For once it's gone, it's gone for good

And promises are cheap…

DON'T SELL OUR SNOWY HYDRO!

The people rise and say!

We gave so much to build her,

Don't throw it all away…

So listen up Australia!

Before it is too late…

If were selling off our water

Then 'God help us', what's our fate…

Never Give Up...

The power of the people show,

We're stronger than we'll ever know,

United, yet again we rose as one...

Australians standing tall and proud,

Our voices echoed long and loud,

We've shown an uphill battle can be won.

Our heritage, our history,

The politicians couldn't see,

Meant so much more than just a balance sheet.

Our power, water, land,

We had to make a stand,

As the 'power brokers' hastily retreat...

The lesson now, I know,

Is to never, ever grow

Too complacent or give up on what is right.

For honest hearts ring true,

Beating strong in me and you,

So we battled on and <u>YES!</u> We won the fight...

Seasons in the Snowy

The rich and vibrant colours
Of another Autumn fall,
Heralding one seasons end,
As natures changes call.

The poplars, so majestic,
Shed their Autumn leaves again,
Floating, dropping all around,
Like sun drenched golden rain.

The maples reds and burgundies,
Amber, green and bronze,
A kaleidoscope of colour,
And slowly baring fronds.

Then subtly the breezes change,
Newness fills the air,
You smell it when the Winter comes,
Grey snow clouds dance with flare.

The snowflakes soon will glisten,
In a rapturous wall of white.
Covering the grass and earth,
In magical delight…

Until the melting of the snow,
When Spring arrives again,
To warm the earth with sun's sweet love,
Where frozen ground had lain.

A menagerie of colour,
Trees and flowers turn to bloom,
The flora and the fauna feast,
They find their bride and groom…

Slowly then the Summer comes,
To heat Monaro plains,
Such warmth and strength enveloping,
The sweetest Summer rains.

The sun enriches from the East,
Endures in the West,
Then at the setting of the sun,
An awe inspiring fest!

A horizontal rainbow,
Will embrace the Eastern sky,
A brilliant scene of colour,
Form and energy on high!

These strong and sacred contrasts,
Fill my being with delight!
The mountains mood, she changes,
Just as day turns in to night.

It may still snow in Summer,
Or be perfect in July,
Four seasons in one day,
In just the blinking of one's eye.

So once again the seasons change,
The wheels of life they turn,
Enduring, never-ending,
Natures lessons, much to learn...

Another year has come and gone,
As predecessors came.
Life's cycles, they continue,
But the memories remain...

Take it Day by Day…

…an ode to Mrs Noreen 'Jack' Pendergast

I wrote this poem at a time when I was really struggling with motherhood, or I thought I was until I heard Jack's story… Her strength and resilience were and still are a true inspiration to me as are so many of the incredible, humble mountain men and women I have been fortunate enough to write about…

I sit here just reflecting on a story I was told,
Imagining a time that's past, a bygone day of old.
We think that life is hard today? Perhaps that's not so true.
I'll share with you this story of a girl I never knew…

She grew up on a country farm, down Snowy River way.
The second child of seven, life was tough back in her day.
She married young, her "new" house just a two room hut of tin.
Gave birth to their first child there, a boy's life forged within.

She raised her own eight children, plus the child of her brother,
In an old brick home, just two bedrooms, all helping one another.
Then suddenly her husband died, her youngest child just five.
She battled on defiantly to keep them all alive.

A life of constant hard work with so very much to do,
No modern cons, no spouse to help, spare moments precious few…
They'd go off to the hills with an old pram collecting wood.
To keep the home fires burning, old stove cooking best it could.

That same old pram would double to take washing to the river.
Summer, Spring or Winter, sometimes swelter, sometimes shiver.
Monday was the wash day, pushing loads through river sand.
The copper and the buckets, all the washing done by hand.

They'd walk up from the river bank, to hang the washing out.
The lines were strung about five deep, some nights you'd hear her shout…
The frost would come and snap the lines, 'twas always quite a fight,
To be out the back propping up the lines on a cold, dark winters night.

There was ironing, mending, sewing, no clothes were dare bought new!
Scrubbing floors and cleaning house, then all the meals too.
The cooking of the Sunday roast, the pudding still to bake,
So ends could meet she'd clean the school, just three pounds ten she'd make.

It's hard to quite imagine such a life of constant grind.
Her resilience amazing, strength of character and mind.
Life has changed immensely and I'm not afraid to say,
Such pioneering Women, there are few like you today…

So stop and smell the eucalypt, see beauty in the sky.
Enjoy and watch our children grow before time passes by…
Appreciate the little things we often just don't see.
Thank those who came before us that we live a life so free...

Now sometimes when I lose my way, don't know which way to turn,
I think about this woman, and the lessons that I learn.
I thank you for your story, for your strong, determined way,
So now I count my blessings and just take it day by day…

A Poem About Autumn

I ought to write a poem
About Autumn I was told.
The days are getting brisker
The nights are turning cold.

The trees are now chameleons
The poplars turn to gold.
A hint of Winter in the air
Now waiting to unfold.

Transition of the seasons
With their tales oh so bold.
A sacred dance since time began
Yet never growing old.

I ought to write a poem
About Autumn I was told.
Natures ever changing beauty
Through mere words we'll not behold…

Our Fate is in Your Hands

This poem was written after many discussions with the locals and in consultation with people such as Leisa Caldwell (Snowy Mountains Horse Riders Association) and Ted Taylor (B.U.G.S. and former member of the P.O.M. Committee). This poem was sent with submissions to a variety of politicians to highlight an issue which underpins the historical importance and cultural identity of so many men and women of the 'High Country'…

An open letter to the politicians of Australia by Lee Taylor-Friend.

The 'winds of change' are blowing, time to rise up and be showing
That the paths our predecessors forged will not be all in vain.
It's time to make a stand and to save this proud southland,
Or a wilderness of heart and soul is all that will remain…

'Plan of Management' are making resolutions now forsaking
The fine history created in this bold and rugged land.
Will you take this precious heritage and burn an all-important bridge
We're building to make way for 'conservation', 'change at hand'?

So much has been forsaken and so very much was taken
When the 'Mighty Snowy River' became just a trickling stream.
And the towns you could not save, buried 'neath a watery grave,
For the feat they called the 'Snowy Scheme'; not everybody's dream…

There is so much you could learn, many kudos you could earn,
Just by listening to the people, to their knowledge, woes and strife.
We need more 'conversation', not just 'blanket conservation',
For they've learnt for generations through the 'grand old school of life'.

'Squeaky wheels get all the oil', lots of bluster, little toil,
Don't be blinded by your 'visions green' and grapple for the vote.
Common sense must now prevail, as we set forth and take sail
On this journey to the future that the history books will note…

Consistency a must, if you wish to gain the trust
Of the people who are struggling with transition and with change.
When the winter hoards arrive, through the 'High Country' they drive
While you slowly ban the locals riding horses on the range.

Have you thought of gas emissions while you're making your submissions,
From the four-wheel drives arriving for the falling of the snow?
Will it be our nations fate, will you lock up the park gate,
And create a 'perfect wilderness' where nobody can go?

For 'The Man From Snowy River', will you stand up and deliver
A fair policy and recognise our heritage, 'so grand'.
It's the lifeblood of our nation, will the 'movement at the station'
Be a 'household word' tomorrow or Australian culture banned?

Understanding must prevail, for we can't afford to fail
Or ignore the precious heritage and history of these lands.
No 'political correctness' should ignore us or reject us.
Will we stay the 'lucky country'? Our fate is in your hands…

Tommys Girl

Mother Snowy – Live or Die

I wrote this poem on the 26th August, 2007, whilst sitting on the banks of the 'Snowy River'. Many in our community had gathered that morning at the Mowamba Weir to commemorate the five year anniversary since the weir was de-commissioned or turned on with great fanfare and media coverage in 2002. It seems all the political grandstanding was for nothing... In 2006 they re-commissioned the weir or turned it off again, denying the Snowy River a natural montane flow. No community consultation was entered in to. Another example of the governments disregard for the people and the river...

NATIONAL TREASURE OR NATIONAL DISGRACE?

Her shallow breath, just audible, she's gasping in her pain.
Sweet memories stir her slumber with a gentle flush of rain.
Her strength and power, all but gone; she's lost so much she bore.
A rich and vibrant entity that almost is no more...

But not because she can't be saved; her life has been deferred.
Is it weakness? Lack of caring? Hearts of stone that won't be stirred?
Were your promises as shallow as the river in her pain?
Will you stand up and be brave enough to give her life again?

Or will money greed and power simply sentence her to die
While the world looks on in horror and they ask the question 'Why?'
Will you silence those that mock you or just laugh, ignore and gloat?
Will you make good on your promises or squeeze her parched, dry throat?

Would you pass a dying stranger, just ignore her gasps for life?
Would you simply not acknowledge your own Mother, Daughter, Wife?
She's a Mother to the ranges; she's a Daughter of the snows,
She's a nurturing Wife and Lover to the land through which she flows.

Will the 'Man from Snowy River' be the 'Man from Snowy Swamp'?
As our river lies there choking while the pollies rant and romp!
Your grand promises were 'plentiful' environmental flow
But she ended up with 'Bugger-all', where did the water go???

How can the people ever trust whilst politicians lie?
They promise 'life eternal', then sentence her to die.
Let's give 'The Snowy' back her life, 'Mowamba Weirs' a start,
When will our river flow again, or don't they have a heart?

Nanna's Chicken Pie

We often expect that nature has a certain order or life has a natural sequence of events but this is not always so. We lost Mum to suicide when I was eight years old. We lost Dad to heart failure back in 1996, but strangely enough we still had my maternal grandparents who were always such a constant in an at times uncertain world.

That changed with the passing of Pop. Just Nan was left, battling on. She'd had so many hurdles to face during her life yet any adversity was always faced with a quiet dignity, putting others before herself with never a complaint or negative word about others.

I dedicate this poem to our wonderful Grandparents who have left a great legacy of fond memories, love and hope…

Sitting on a Sunday, I reflect on days gone by,
Sweet and subtle memories, another place and time…
As children the excitement mounts, for now the time draws nigh,
Time to visit Nan and Pop, and Nannas' chicken pie!

A family trip on Sundays, the highlight of the week,
Mum and Dad, Cath and Mick and two girls each a piece.
Most times we'd go in Aunt Cath's car, and over bridge we'd travel.
Arriving soon at Nan and Pop's, the day would thus unravel…

We'd all run in excitedly to hug our Nan and Pop,
We'd chat about the week gone by, admire Pop's vegie crop.
We'd race to the small swimming pool, we'd splash and laugh and play,
Warm weather, free and easy times, such happy, happy days…

In cooler months the swimming pool instead was filled with sand,
Barrowed, shovelled, bucketed, all by Pop's own hand,
We'd run and play and throw the ball and clamber on the fence,
We'd steer clear of that 'foxy' dog; we'd use our common sense.

Grey weatherboards, brick out-house with a horseshoe and a nail,
We'd throw the horseshoe wildly, miss most times without fail,
The vegie patch resplendent, the choko vine sublime,
The Spackmans' in the big back house, another place and time...

Then lunchtime came, we'd run inside, all seated, saint or sinner,
The clattering of knives and forks and the chorus 'We want dinner!!!'
The wafting of delicious food, the laughter, chitter-chatter,
Those things have all been lost today, the things that really matter...

Then piping hot the pie arrived, we'd all be served our share,
That tasty pie so succulent, to get seconds, truly rare!
Rice pudding was our main dessert, but try though as I may,
I've never quite perfected it, can't make it Nanna's way...

When lunch was done, the cards came out, the adults they would play,
Mostly eucha or five-hundred, for loose change, to fill the day.
The kids would play or sometimes we would have a sing-a-long,
Pop played his old accordion with a passion loud and strong...

But time marched on, our lives all changed, those Sundays became few,
But still I look back fondly on a time a child knew...
Days of love and days of fun, all mixed with the odd tear,
Days we lived so wild and free, we had no time for fear.

No longer in that same old house with weatherboards of grey,
Pop lost a hard fought battle; Nan too has passed away...
Times so sweet and special fade...with the blinking of one's eye,
Days of love and laughter – and Nanna's chicken pie...

High Country Dreams...

This poem was chosen as one of five Australian finalists for the Australian Bush Laureate Awards 2009 'Bush Poem of the year'. A great honour indeed...

As the noble boughs are swaying on the gum trees by the door
And the winter winds are echoed 'cross the hills.
I sit and write, reflecting on the journey that has been.
With the warmth of new found friendships my heart fills...

'Twas a calling to the Mountains, to a different way of life
And a chance to start our city life anew.
Down by the Snowy River with the distant snow-capped ranges
The sweet splendour of the 'High Country' just grew...

But the beauty of the mountains doesn't just lie in the landscape
Or the ethereal visions of a distant view.
It's a true and lasting beauty that the eye cannot behold
And a gift that just cannot be bought, it's true...

It's the beauty of the people; it's the passion in their souls.
It's the staunch and stoic humble mountain way.
It's the battling through the hard times, the rejoicing in the good
And the helping of a mate who's gone astray...

It's supporting your community; pitch in when times are tough,
Or volunteer to help a local cause.
It's the group participation, raising funds for someone needy
And the comfort of the 'always open doors'...

Tommys Girl

It's 'My Mate Jack' who's eighty-nine and shares his precious yarns
As he says 'Come, sit, I'll tell you some more lies!'
His face lights up, his chest swells, as he talks about the past
And his memories of the war bring misty eyes…

It's my dear friend Jackie Jackson – she's a real life inspiration.
She is always there to lend a helping hand.
She's got five kids of her own, but you never hear her groan,
And her smile and laughter leave a lasting brand…

It's the 'characters', the 'larrikins', the wry bush sense of humour,
That always seems to strike a special chord.
History, heritage and pride, the legend never died.
It's why the Banjos 'Man' is so adored…

Now we're raising our two children on our farm here in the country,
Such a contrast from the streets where I grew up.
The city life of Redfern seems a million miles away
Where I played and strayed when I was just a pup…

But for those who said 'Sheer Madness!' when we said 'We're going bush'
You can see it's not as crazy as it seems.
Our lives have been transformed, inspired, enriched beyond belief
As we now live out our true 'High Country Dreams'…

I'm Home...

I guess this poem really sums up what the mountains mean to me...

I
love
this mountain
country, a land of
many moods, engrossing and
uplifting, she ebbs, she flows, she broods.

Her
rugged
sacred beauty
seen from battlements
on high, that mystic mountain
majesty that captures heart and eye.

The
sun embracing
snow gums ethereal
imagery, dawn break.
Enduring skies sweet canopy,
strong earth that won't forsake.

A
natures
song so graceful
sung by birds of every
wing, her whispers echoed
perfectly by every living thing.

The
sunlight
glistens on blue
lakes all made by
natures hand. Such cool sweet
glacial waters mirror images so grand.

These
mountains
that surround me
as I walk along this shore,
evoke a strange, sweet knowingness,
My hearts been here before...

The
South lands'
in my very soul,
and there it shall remain,
for once it gets into your blood,
life's not the same again...

With
every
fibre of my being,
wherever I may roam,
I love this mountain country
and it's here that I call home.

Time

For Shaaron and Bill

Time so precious comes and goes

but to where nobody knows…

Memories filled with love and hope

help our hearts and souls to cope.

Whispering wind on gentle breeze

etched in ice that time doth freeze…